ANGKOR
A Tour of the Monuments

Text by **Thierry Zéphir**

Photography by **Luca Invernizzi Tettoni**

Translation by **Milton Osborne**

ARCHIPELAGO PRESS

For Albert Le Bonheur

The author acknowledges his special thanks
to **Pierre-Yves Manguin** and **Pierre Baptiste**.

All photographs are by **Luca Invernizzi Tettoni**, with the exception of :

Achilleus: pages 6, 17 (bottom left), 18 (top), 20 (top), 27 (top right), 36 (top right), 38 (top right), 43 (top left), 49 (top right, centre right), 60 (bottom), 62 (bottom), 64, 65 (top right, top left, bottom right), 66 (top left), 69, 70 (top), 71 (middle centre, middle right, bottom left, bottom right)
Marie-Claude Millet: pages 65 (bottom left), 70 (bottom)
Photobank: page 71 (top right)

Cover photographs
Front: Angkor Wat.
Back, left to right: *devata* at Banteay Srei; a Bayon bas-relief; *devata* at Ta Prohm.

Copyright © 2004 Editions Didier Millet

First published in 2004 by **Archipelago Press**
an imprint of **Editions Didier Millet**
121 Telok Ayer Street, #03–01
Singapore 068590

www.edmbooks.com

Editor: **Shan Wolody**
Designer: **Nelani Jinadasa**
Maps: **Anuar Bin Abdul Rahim**
Production Manager: **Sin Kam Cheong**

Colour separation by SC Graphics, Singapore
Printed in Singapore by Tien Wah Press Pte Ltd

ISBN: 981-4068-73-X

CONTENTS

Introduction

4

Angkor Wat

10

Angkor Thom and
Its Monuments

22

Around
Angkor Thom

40

Away from
Angkor

58

Map of the Sites

72

Map of Angkor Thom

74

Glossary

75

Bibliography

76

From very rare historical accounts, a few fleeting 'snapshots' among bas-relief carvings, but above all from an architectural heritage that is unique in the world, we have a testimony to the brilliance of Khmer civilisation at the time when Angkor, the ancient Yashodharapura, was the most powerful empire ever to exist in Southeast Asia. As in the past, when it was the historic capital of Cambodia, Angkor (a name derived phonetically from the Sanskrit *nagara*, meaning a town or city, modified as *nokor* and then as *angkor*) is once again a magnet for many visitors. The prestige of the site comes both from the splendour of the monuments and the very special

INTRODUCTION

character of their setting, which juxtaposes plains and hills, forests and rice fields, lakes and watercourses. In this pleasingly diverse landscape, the Khmers themselves, who have lived here since the earliest times, are the greatest of all the riches at Angkor. This human richness and its timeless culture gives Angkor its true soul. No matter how long a visitor spends here, and however little one strays from the beaten track, the sight of a Buddhist ceremony in a modest village pagoda or of a fisherman pulling in his line is what reflects the clear cultural continuity of this site, far more than all the studies produced by scholars.

Not so long ago, at the beginning of the 20th century, Cambodians believed that these fabled temples were built on the order of the gods by the celestial architect, Pisnukar. The legend tells how, at the dawn of time, Prince Preah Ket Mealea, the natural son of the Hindu god Indra and a human woman, visited his father's heavenly palace; how, as a result of the admiration shown by the young man for the marvels he saw during his visit to the celestial world, Indra offered him the Kingdom of Cambodia and said he would build for him there whatever monument he desired from among those he saw. Then, the legend continues, Preah Ket Mealea, fearing he might seem impudent if he chose Indra's own palace, modestly asked only for a replica of the heavenly

domain's cattle stable; finally, Pisnukar made a model of the building in a single night and covered it with a magic glaze that transformed it into stone. The legend of Preah Ket Mealea and the creation of Angkor Wat, preserves in the names of the main actors—Indra and Pisnukar, that is, Vishvakarman, the architect of the gods in Hindu mythology—the memory of a past full of Indian cultural ideas and values. It is this distant past that scholarly research has rescued from oblivion since the West's discovery of Angkor in the middle of the 19th century. In Cambodia, of course, the monuments had never been forgotten. What they represented, their origin and their purpose, were no longer understood, but they were not forgotten. For the West, on the other hand, the discovery of the monuments was a revelation. The missionaries, to begin with, were puzzled by the strangeness of the buildings that some of them saw briefly in the 16th century. The travellers and other explorers of the 19th century, such as Henry Mouhot (1826–1861), were fascinated by these enormous buildings half buried under vegetation. This was when France undertook a task commensurate with its presence in Southeast Asia by studying the countries over which it had extended its control: Vietnam, Laos and Cambodia. The real achievement of the École française d'Extrême-Orient, established in 1898, is found in the outstanding work of the architects, restorers, epigraphists and art historians who opened up a totally virgin field of knowledge and formed the framework of research for all modern study of Khmer civilisation.

For convenience, if somewhat artificially since there is no clear-cut break between one period and another, it is customary to subdivide the history of Cambodia into three major periods. The names given to these periods underline the importance of the ancient Cambodian capital in the eyes of historians and in terms of the country's development. The 'pre-Angkorian' period covers the first centuries of the Christian era to the end of the 8th century and was a time that saw the emergence of a classical Khmer civilisation that reached its apogee in the succeeding period. This first period is often spoken of as a time of 'Indianisation' and was characterised by the adoption—but also to a considerable extent by the adaptation to local needs and to a cultural sub-strata that has been shown by recent research to have been very important—of basic elements of Indian culture: religions, languages, conceptions of royalty, to note the most important. The 'Angkorian' period (802–1431) is defined by the ideas already adopted from India coming into full effect, and by the implementation of a highly centralised system of government which reproduced the symbolic organisation of the world of the gods in the world of men. The king was at the top of the social system, ensuring the kingdom's prosperity and the well-being of his subjects, in the same way as the supreme divinity, whoever this was according to the ruler's choice of religion, ensured the maintenance of the cosmic order from his place at the highest of all the celestial spheres. The 'Post-Angkorian' period begins with the abandonment of Angkor as Cambodia's capital, traditionally said to have occurred in 1431. If the abandonment of Angkor by Cambodia's royalty represents, to some extent, an historical break with the past, this was certainly not the case from a cultural point of view. For it was during the 14th century when there was a major religious change that we really see the transition from Angkorian to modern Cambodia. At that time, the abandonment of the elite religions of Brahmanism (or Hinduism) and Mahayana Buddhism (Greater Vehicle Buddhism) in favour of Theravada

Buddhism (Lesser Vehicle Buddhism)—an event matched by the abandonment of Sanskrit as the language of culture and religion in favour of Pali—was of much greater cultural and historical significance than the simple departure from the capital.

From the prehistoric period to the historical period, Cambodia's cultural development was comparable to that of other Southeast Asian countries such as Thailand, notably, where archeological research is currently more advanced. The Angkor region to the north of the Tonle Sap—the Great Lake which is an inexhaustible source of fish and which triples its area during the rainy season from 3,000 square kilometres to 10,000 square kilometres—provided a favourable habitat for man from neolithic times. The initial knowledge that we have of Angkor and the region around it comes, essentially, from excavations, both those carried out some time ago and others undertaken more recently that await detailed publication. A number of sites in the Roluos area studied in the 1960s seem to have been occupied from around 1000 BCE. More recently, some 'round towns', large settlements in circular form surrounded by an earth levee, have been found in the Angkor region. These are characteristic of a period a little before Indianisation took place in the countries of mainland Southeast Asia. To the west of the Western Baray (a *baray* is a reservoir), little remains today of a group of monuments dating from the pre-Angkorian period (7th–8th centuries). And a town site laid out in square form, most of which disappeared when the *baray* was constructed in the 11th century, was the location for various temples of which the most important, Prasat Ak Yum, is a stepped pyramid, the earliest known example of a temple-mountain.

With the accession to power of Jayavarman II (reigned 802 to after 830?), who was anointed in a solemn ceremony on Phnom Kulen, to the north of Angkor, the Khmer kingdom entered the mature stage of its development. Freeing the kingdom from control by 'Java'—a kingdom whose exact location is still unknown— and unifying its scattered territories, Jayavarman II set in train various rituals that are recorded in inscriptions, such as the cult of the *devaraja* which

BELOW: Prasat Ak Yum (7th–8th centuries) is the earliest true temple-mountain found at Angkor. It was incorporated in the southern dyke of the Western Baray during the latter's construction in the 11th century. A Shaivite brick monument, today it is in a ruined state. At the time it was constructed Prasat Ak Yum had three terraces, of which only two can partly be seen today. On the second terrace there were four sanctuary towers— one at each corner—as well as various other minor buildings (perhaps a total of eight), all constructed in brick. The main sanctuary tower was built on the third terrace, but little of this structure remains today. A 12-metre-deep shaft leading to the foundations of the building ends under the cella of the sanctuary tower in an underground vault whose exact purpose is uncertain.

ABOVE: Phnom Bakheng (late 9th to early 10th centuries), the eastern façade of the pyramid. The first Angkorian city under King Yashovarman (reigned 889 to early 10th century) had the Phnom Bakheng hill at its centre, with its summit the site for one of the most complex monuments at Angkor. This Shaivite temple—which echoed the form of Mount Meru, the axis of the universe in Indian cosmography—had not less than 109 sanctuary towers.

underlined the importance of the god Shiva as the protector of the country and the guarantor of prosperity. Our knowledge of this event comes from the study and interpretation of inscriptions on stone, the only Cambodian written documents available to us. Written in Sanskrit and old Khmer, the roughly 1,200 known inscriptions so far studied reveal the complexity and richness of the religious world with which they are almost exclusively concerned. Apart from these historical documents, other sources—especially Chinese ones, among which particular mention must be made of the late but very valuable eyewitness account of Zhou Daguan, written at the end of the 13th century—provide a range of important and often very precise information complementing the official material found in the epigraphic record. Jayavarman's last place of residence, the city of Hariharalaya (present-day Roluos, some 15 kilometres east of Siem Reap) remained the capital under his two immediate successors: Jayavarman III, about whom we know little, and Indravarman (r. 877 to at least 886). This latter ruler was, according to inscriptions, associated with various foundations at the Roluos site: a *baray* dating from 877, which was a vast reservoir of water surrounded by dykes that irrigated areas below it through

a system of canals; the Preah Ko temple, consecrated in 879, which established a cult to Shiva and his consort for the benefit of Indravarman's royal predecessors on the throne; and, finally, the Bakong temple-mountain, consecrated in 881, where the god Shiva, in the abstract form of a *linga*, was venerated as the kingdom's protector. Indravarman's successor, Yashovarman (r. 889–after 900?), after having founded the Lolei temple at Roluos in 893, ordered the construction of Yashodharatataka, the present Eastern Baray at Angkor, and founded some 100 centres for religious teaching, the Yashodharashrama, as well as the Phnom Bakheng temple on one of the few hills in the Angkor region. This temple became the centre of his capital, present-day Angkor.

Following the reign of two further rulers, Jayavarman IV came to the throne (r. 928–c. 940) and moved his capital about 100 kilometres northeast of Angkor to the present-day site of Koh Ker. With the accession to the throne of King Rajendravarman (r. 944–967), Cambodia's royal and religious institutions returned to Angkor, where they remained until the abandonment of the capital after 1431. This great ruler, who led a victorious military campaign against Champa—an Indianised kingdom located in the centre and south of modern Vietnam which was

often at war with the Khmer kingdom—around 950, built the Eastern Mebon temple in 953, and the Pre Rup temple in 961. During his reign, much more than had previously been the case, the importance of the kingdom's great dignitaries, both Brahmans and military leaders, was affirmed and continued to increase subsequently. It was one of these dignitaries who built the celebrated temple of Ishvarapura, better known nowadays as Banteay Srei. This was the temple where the restoration technique known as 'anastylosis' was first used. The technique involves rebuilding a temple with its original, displaced

stones on firm foundations, then filling in gaps with new materials. Under Jayavarman V (r. 968–1000 or 1001) a number of monuments were built that cannot be dated precisely: Ta Keo, the Khleangs, and the *gopura* (entrance gateway) of the Royal Palace. It was precisely here, in the area around the palace where the Phimeanakas temple is now located, that recent excavations have revealed foundations, perhaps dating back to the reign of Yashovarman I. The 11th century began with a time of troubles marked by a succession of weak kings. Following a civil war, Suryavarman I (r. 1010–1049) came to the throne in 1010, although he claimed in his inscriptions to have acceded to power in 1002. He made many foundations away from the capital but the only building at Angkor linked to his reign was the vaulted sandstone gallery on the third storey of the Phimeanakas temple. This was an important innovation for the later development of architecture at Angkor. Udayadityavarman II (r. 1050–1066) built the Baphuon temple, undertook or completed the construction of the Western Baray and founded the Western Mebon temple at the very centre of this immense reservoir measuring eight kilometres from east to west and 2.2 kilometres from north to south. It was here, in 1936, that the remains of a reclining Vishnu, the biggest bronze Khmer statue ever discovered, were found. From

1066 to 1113 three rulers succeeded each other without constructing any important monuments at Angkor.

A complex set of developments surrounded the accession to the throne of Suryavarman II (r. 1113 to at least 1145). The founder of Angkor Wat, he set himself apart from almost all the kings of Cambodia before him by his embrace of the Vaishnavite faith. Of an ambitious nature, he mounted several military campaigns against Champa and the Kingdom of Lavo (present-day Lopburi in modern Thailand), and during his reign the Khmer empire expanded more widely than had been the case under any of his predecessors. The construction of Angkor Wat marked the beginning of the most brilliant chapter in the history of Angkorian architecture. The period that followed Suryavarman II's reign was complex and difficult. It ended with the seizure of Angkor by the invading Chams in 1177. Resistance against the invaders was organised over a period of four years and once the reconquest of Angkor was achieved Jayavarman VII, the last great ruler of the Angkorian period (r. 1181–1218?), was anointed as king. At this time there was an important change in the field of religion. Both in terms of the king's own faith and in the light of the Hindu gods' failure to prevent the fall of Angkor to the Chams, Greater Vehicle Buddhism (Mahayana Buddhism) was adopted as the state religion. Nevertheless, Jayavarman VII did not turn his back on the past entirely and Hindu gods still had an important part in the religious life of the time.

Under Jayavarman VII Angkor Thom was enclosed within a wall and many monuments of major importance were consecrated, notably Ta Prohm, Preah Khan and the Bayon. The founding of these temples went hand in hand with a major program for the reform of the Khmer empire: the construction and upgrading of the road system, the establishment of way houses and of hospitals. Jayavarman VII's achievements, about which an inscription says that 'he suffers the pain of his subjects more than his own pain', were completed with military conquests that extended the empire's frontiers far beyond those established by Suryavarman II. Jayavarman VII's second successor, Jayavarman VIII (r. 1243–1295), reinstated the worship of Shiva as the

state religion, apparently as a reaction to the changes imposed by his predecessor. Under Shrindravarman (r. 1295–1307)—whose reign is best known for having been the time when the Chinese embassy, accompanied by Zhou Daguan, visited Angkor—Lesser Vehicle Buddhism (Theravada Buddhism) greatly increased its influence, setting in train the most important cultural and religious change in Cambodia's history.

From the middle of the 14th century Cambodia was involved in a series of conflicts with Siam. Armies from the Kingdom of Ayutthaya seized Angkor at various times until the city was finally abandoned following the removal from power of King Dhammashokaraja in 1431. From this time Angkor ceased to be the capital and was only temporarily reoccupied for a brief period in the 16th century. During this reoccupation a number of important building projects were carried out, such as the construction of large Buddha statues—though these were not completed—at Phnom Bakheng, Baphuon and Tep Pranam temples, as well as the completion of two bas-reliefs on the northeast quadrant of the third enclosure gallery of Angkor Wat.

Although Angkor is no longer the capital of the Khmer state, it nevertheless remains its most powerful and tangible symbol. With further archeological excavations to take place, the years ahead promise a rich harvest of information that will allow us to gain a much more precise understanding of the site and its history than is possible today.

LEFT: Windows with balusters and *devata*.

BELOW: A view from the external dyke of the 190-metre-wide moat surrounding Angkor Wat. The western causeway provides the main entrance to the monument. The central structure is linked to the monument's lateral carriage gates, the elephant gates, by a majestic gallery.

ANGKOR WAT

The city that became a temple

Without doubt, Angkor Wat, in company with Borobudur in Java, is the best-known monument in Southeast Asia, a fact justified by its formal architectural perfection, the quality of its decoration and its harmonious and balanced proportions. The temple perfectly summarises Khmer architectural genius, so much so that people often refer to it as 'the Angkor temple' as if there is only one. Of course, this is not the case, but if it were necessary to visit only one temple, this would be it.

The temple was constructed in a sustained burst of energy during the first half of the reign of King Suryavarman II (r. 1113 to at least 1145). Dedicated to Vishnu, one of the three great Hindu gods along with Shiva and Brahma, it faces west, an orientation that has been the cause of some controversy. But this particular characteristic of the temple simply places it on a par with the western orientation of some Vaishnavite temples in India, a positioning laid down

in various standard architectural treatises that, one way or another, the Khmers must have known about. It has also been suggested that the orientation reflects the temple having a funerary character. While it is possible that Suryavarman II's ashes were placed in the monument after his cremation, it certainly is not the case that the temple is a mausoleum built to the glory of this great ruler in the afterworld. Such an idea simply does not fit in with what we know about the ancestor cults of Angkorian Cambodia. Angkor Wat belongs to that category of temple-mountains—monuments constructed in the form of stepped pyramids—sheltering in the main sanctuary tower (*prasat* in Khmer) the protecting divinity of the kingdom whose nature and name could change from one reign to another. The rich symbolism of this kind of monument is related to Indian concepts of a temple as an actual microcosm, reproducing in the world of men the physical arrangements of the homes of the gods in the heavens. Since in India and in the Indianised countries of Southeast Asia these homes are believed to be mountains, it is possible to understand fully the role of these Khmer monuments. They furnished the gods with a place where they would be ready to reside on earth to help human beings and to guarantee their prosperity. With its five *prasat* at the third level of the pyramid, its four concentric enclosures and its moats, Angkor Wat is in every way the ideal model of the god Vishnu's heavenly abode.

Angkor Wat

A model of architectural composition

Built in the form of four concentric enclosures, Angkor Wat represents the ultimate achievement of the principles of composition developed by Khmer architects following the pre-Angkorian period. Starting from a central module, in this case the main sanctuary tower of the pyramid, the constituent parts of the temple—sanctuary towers, access pavilions, libraries, and so on—are organised in a rigorous fashion according to a very strict orthogonal pattern. Along an imaginary line following the major east–west axis of the temple, each aspect of the northern half is matched symmetrically in the southern half. Viewed in elevation, the horizontal aspect provided at different levels of the monument by the galleries is counterbalanced by the vertical lines of the sanctuary towers, guiding the eye towards the uppermost point of the central tower some 60 metres above ground level. Even today, despite the loss of some superstructure at the western entrance and the second enclosure gallery, the temple still provides an impression of perfect architectural balance.

PREVIOUS PAGES, LEFT: The western entrance seen from the cruciform terrace at the base of the pyramid.

PREVIOUS PAGES, RIGHT: Two of the many *devata* or *apsara* which decorate the walls. Some of the most richly dressed and adorned, as here, are found on the eastern façade of the western entrance.

TOP, LEFT: One of the six flights of stone steps lined with *naga* balustrades leading from the western entrance to the base of the pyramid. In the background is the southern library within the fourth enclosure.

CENTRE, LEFT: Whether as individuals or groups, the *devata* at Angkor Wat present an extraordinary range of hairstyles.

BOTTOM, LEFT: The damned; a detail of the bas-relief known as 'Heaven and Hell' in the eastern wing of the southern bas-relief gallery (see pages 18–19).

RIGHT: The pyramid, viewed from the southwest from within the fourth enclosure.

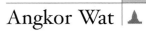

Angkor Wat

From Vishnu to Buddha

Originally consecrated to the god Vishnu, the temple's dedication was changed so that it became a Buddhist sanctuary at a later, and still uncertain, date. Paradoxically, this symbol of the triumph of Hindu religion has become one of the most important Buddhist monuments in Cambodia. The signs of the change in religious affiliation of the temple are most clearly seen at the level of the central sanctuary tower, where doorways were walled up to provide locations for statues of the Buddha, and at the level of the cruciform courtyard. The novel system of galleries supported by pillars makes it possible to pass under cover from the first to the second level of the pyramid on its western side. The interior surfaces of these vaults were covered by deeply recessed wooden ceilings ornamented by lotus flowers in bloom. The disappearance of these ceilings gives the galleries a quite different set of proportions to what had been imagined by those who conceived this construction. The cruciform courtyard shelters a number of statues from varying periods. There was a more important collection previously, but the vindictive Khmer Rouge vented their rage against the Buddhist religion and its symbols here.

LEFT: The cruciform courtyard is formed by two galleries with pillars intersecting at right angles; some late inscriptions (16th century and later) are found on some of these.
ABOVE, TOP: A *devata*.

ABOVE: A Buddha protected by a *naga* in the Preah Ko style (last quarter of the 9th century) in the first enclosure gallery at the third level.
RIGHT: Buddha images (14th century and later) in the south wing of the cruciform courtyard.

▲ Angkor Wat – Bas-reliefs

On the walls, the legends of the gods

If it is possible to glimpse the trace of a narrative composition on the fourth terrace of the Bakong pyramid, which was consecrated in 881, Angkor Wat, built some 300 years later, is where the art of the narrative bas-relief reaches its apogee. In the third enclosure gallery, at the first level of the pyramid, there are eight great panels, covering a total length of some 520 metres and with a height of two metres, that present episodes drawn from Indian epics (the great battles of Lanka and Kurukshetra from the *Ramayana* and the *Mahabharata*, in the western gallery) and various sacred texts (the churning of the sea of milk from the *Bhagavata-purana*, in the eastern gallery). Beside these mythological scenes, the bas-reliefs of the southern gallery illustrate, first, an historical procession with various individuals identified by short inscriptions, notably Suryavarman II, under his posthumous name of Paramavishnuloka, and, second, the rewards and punishments after death, the scenes known as 'Heaven and Hell'. These bas-reliefs, which at first seem confusing, are composed with consummate skill both spatially and in terms of perspective through about a dozen successive planes with a narrative logic articulated along strong lines either obliquely or in a zigzag fashion. The scenes depicted on the bas-reliefs either have a metronomic regularity (the churning of the sea of milk) or, in contrast, are free and exuberant in character (the battles of Lanka and Kurukshetra). The traces of coloured paint found on some panels are from a later period, but it is likely that at the time the bas-reliefs were executed some, at least, were painted and gilded.

TOP, LEFT: This bas-relief illustrates the churning of the sea of milk by the *deva* (gods) and the *asura* (demons) to produce *amrita* (the liquor of immortality). The churning was achieved by using the serpent Vasuki that the gods and demons wound around Mount Mandara. The mountain was thrust into the depths of the sea of milk and stabilised by Vishnu, in the form of a tortoise. In the upper area of the panel there are *apsara* who were created by the churning even before the liquor of immortality appeared.
FAR LEFT: Two feminine beings in a detail from the 'Heaven and Hell' bas-reliefs in the eastern wing of the southern gallery.
LEFT: Khmer foot-soldiers in armour: a detail from the 'Historical Procession' in the western wing of the southern gallery.

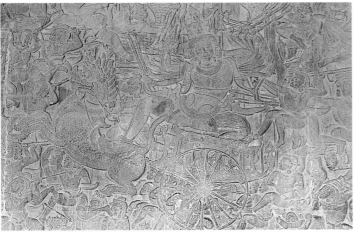

TOP, LEFT: The demon Ravana, in the northern wing of the western gallery. The Battle of Lanka at the end of the *Ramayana* was a major engagement between Rama and his monkey allies and the *rakshasa*, a particular kind of demon, who were led by their chief, the terrible multi-headed and multi-armed Ravana.

TOP, RIGHT: According to the inscription accompanying this scene from the 'Historical Procession' in the western wing of the southern gallery, this is 'The Supreme Person, the Sacred Feet, My Lord Paramavishnuloka, seated on Mount Shivapada, receiving the homage of his troops.' This complicated formula describes Suryavarman II under his posthumous name. This name indicates that the king has gone to the abode (*loka*) of the supreme (*parama*) Vishnu. The inscription, dating from the 12th century, was obviously not engraved until after the death of the ruler.

LEFT: The goal of the Battle of Lanka was to free Rama's consort, Sita, who had been abducted by Ravana. In the centre of this picture, Rama is standing on Hanuman, the bravest of the monkeys, loosing his victorious arrows. Rama is accompanied by his brother, Lakshmana, and by Vibhihsana, Ravana's own brother, who has rejoined the side of goodness. With his demonic appearance, his hairstyle distinguishes him from the others.

Phnom Bakheng, Baksei Chamkrong, Prasat Bei

The centre of the first Angkor

The capital of Yashovarman I at the end of the 9th century was established on one of the few hills in the Angkor region, Phnom Bakheng. The temple built on the top of this hill represented Mount Meru, the axis of the world in Hindu cosmography and the home of all the gods. The arrangement of the towers on the summit matches the traditional descriptions of Mount Meru, with a central tower rising high above its base counterbalanced by four smaller monuments at the corners of the terrace. Prasat Bei (middle of the 10th century) and Baksei Chamkrong are located to the north of Phnom Bakheng. Founded some time between 912 and 922 by Harshavarman I, Baksei Chamkrong was repaired by Rajendravarman in 948. It is in the form of a temple-mountain representing Mount Kailasa, situated to the northwest of Mount Meru according to the Hindu texts—this is exactly the location of Baksei Chamkrong in relation to Phnom Bakheng.

RIGHT: An aerial view of Phnom Bakheng. The temple has 109 *prasat* located around the pyramid and on its five terraces. The builders of this monument did not hesitate to construct a large number of sandstone structures on the pyramid itself—12 small subsidiary temples on each terrace, five majestic towers on the summit—because, in contrast to all the other temple-mountains, its internal core consists of the rock of the hill itself on which it was constructed.

BELOW: The eastern façade of the Phnom Bakheng pyramid. The god Shiva was worshipped in the form of a *linga* in the central sanctuary tower on the fifth terrace of the pyramid. The *prasat* on the summit have suffered considerable damage, notably during construction of a base for a monumental Buddha image at the top of the temple—never completed—probably dating from the 16th century.

RIGHT: The style of the small columns and lintels framing the doors of Prasat Bei's three brick sanctuary towers dates this monument to the beginning of Rajendravarman's reign (around 950) or even slightly earlier.
BELOW, RIGHT: The eastern façade of Baksei Chamkrong. A skilful, progressive reduction in the proportions of the different component parts of this temple dedicated to Shiva gives it elegance and a special sense of balance.

In 1181 Jayavarman VII mounted the throne and ushered in one of the most active periods in Angkor's history. The dramatic historical circumstances preceding and accompanying the king's rise to power—the seizure of Angkor by the Chams in 1177, and internal revolts—doubtless explain and justify the important political and religious changes that then took place. In historical terms, Jayavarman appears to have been both ambitious and energetic, a great military leader, and a skilled diplomat. He liberated his country from the Chams who had occupied it

ANGKOR THOM AND ITS MONUMENTS

During the reign of Jayavarman VII the Angkorian landscape was changed for the last time

since 1177, he greatly extended Cambodia's frontiers to the west, to the present border between Burma and Thailand, and to the north, as far as Vientiane in modern-day Laos. And he reduced Champa to the status of a Khmer province for some 20 years. A Buddhist by family tradition, and doubtless also by personal conviction, Jayavarman made Mahayana Buddhism the state religion. Many inscriptions testify to the importance of religious works carried out by the ruler and various members of the royal family. An inscription at the Phimeanakas temple, for instance, illuminates the activities of the royal wives, dealing as it does with Jayavarman's much-loved principal consort, Jayarajadevi, and her elder sister, Indradevi, who was both the author of the inscription and who succeeded her sister as the king's principal wife after her death. An innovator in many areas, Jayavarman also looked to the past as he governed, recognising the wisdom of taking advice from Brahmans. In the final analysis, his reign was a novel synthesis of the religious, institutional, economic and political history of Cambodia rather than any sort of cultural revolution. In terms of architecture, the period is marked throughout the country by a large number of new foundations, both royal and otherwise, so that it is often said that more temples were constructed throughout Cambodia during this one reign than during all the previous reigns. The most important architectural complex at Angkor, Angkor Thom, is composed of the Bayon (the last Angkorian temple-mountain); the moats and 12-kilometre-long walls surrounding the city; the impressive entrance gateways adorned with faces that provide access to the city; as well as important modifications to the Royal Palace (interior pools) and its immediate surroundings (the Elephant Terrace and the Terrace of the Leper King). But these works, dating from the end of the 12th century and the beginning of the 13th century, added to, and in some cases were superimposed upon, a pre-existing complex dating back to at least the beginning of the Angkorian period. For it seems that this area of Angkor had always been accorded great importance. The Royal Palace—whose surrounding wall and *gopura* probably date from the end of the 10th century or the earliest years of the 11th century—provides eloquent testimony of this: apart from the modifications and additions from Jayavarman VII's time, there are architectural components, that undoubtedly have been reused, dating from the end of the 10th century. An example is a lintel, still in place, on the southern face of the almost completely collapsed sanctuary tower of the Phimeanakas. Elsewhere, and looking back over the centuries, the following temples reveal Angkor Thom's complex character: Preah Palilay (12th–13th centuries), Baphuon (third quarter of the 11th century), the north and south Khleangs (end of the 10th century), and directly to the east of the north Khleang a small monument in the style of Banteay Srei (third quarter of the 10th century). The beginning of the 13th century did not see an end to the evolution of the Angkor Thom site. Various changes were made to existing buildings, notably to the Bayon. The latest of the monuments, such as Prasat Suor Prat, the Preah Pithu group, the Mangalartha temple or monument 486, bring us to at least the 16th century.

Gates of Angkor Thom

The faces of the guardian kings protect the city

The wall surrounding Angkor Thom forms a square, each side three kilometres long and with a height of about eight metres, enclosing Jayavarman VII's city. It was both defensive and symbolic in character. A pathway ran along its top and at each corner of the wall was a small temple, the Prasat Chrung, each one containing an inscription praising the ruler. A 100-metre-wide moat surrounded the outside of this wall and could only be crossed at five locations by causeways, each lined by 54 giants, with benevolent faces along the left-hand side and with fearsome faces on the right-hand side. These giants hold an enormous many-headed *naga* whose heads, displayed in an arch-like form, welcome a visitor. It has been suggested that the giants are involved in churning the sea of milk, conceived on the scale of the whole of the city, but it is also possible that the giants and the *naga* are simply guardians of the city. Besides, the faces on the gates have been identified as those of the kings who are guardians of the cardinal points, keeping watch over the city.

TOP, RIGHT: Giants with fearsome faces on the southern causeway.
RIGHT: The southern gate seen from outside the city. As a visitor approaches Angkor Thom, the faces of the kings who are guardians of the cardinal points appear as if by magic among the trees. Watching over the city, the gates are also linked to Indra, the king of the gods, whose image is displayed at each side of the gate mounted on his three-headed elephant, Airavata.
OPPOSITE PAGE
TOP, LEFT: The western gate seen from outside the city. Here, as is the case with the Gate of the Dead, the causeway of giants has not been restored.
TOP, CENTRE: The northern gate.
TOP, RIGHT: The Gate of the Dead, one of two gates on the eastern side of Angkor Thom's surrounding wall, is in line with the Bayon temple, itself at the centre of the city.
BELOW: The other gate on the eastern side of the wall around Angkor Thom is the Gate of Victory, seen here from the pathway along the top of the wall. It is displaced slightly towards the north in relation to the east–west median axis of the city and is in line with the main entrance to the Royal Palace.

Bayon

The assembly hall for all the gods

Set at the heart of Angkor Thom, the Bayon is a striking three-tiered temple which may be seen as the 'Hall of Proper Conduct' in which the gods gathered from time to time to be taught by the Buddha under the protection of the eternally youthful Brahmanic deities who form part of the Buddhist cosmos. Their faces adorn the 49 sanctuary towers of the second and third levels of the monument. While not all specialists agree with this interpretation, it seems more satisfactory than those that suggest these are the faces of Lokeshvara or Vajrapani (two important divinities in Greater Vehicle Buddhism), the Buddha himself, or the king. As with many of Jayavarman VII's foundations, the Bayon underwent various alterations both during its construction and subsequently. The complex plan of the temple and the impression of confusion a visitor experiences result as much from these alterations as from the very large number of gods that were intended to be installed in the cellae and entrance ways of the sanctuary towers. The principal statue, an image of the Buddha sheltered by a *naga*, was found in 1933 in the course of an excavation of the foundations below the central cella. Today it is housed in a pavilion built for it on an ancient Buddhist terrace immediately to the east of the southern group of the Prasat Suor Prat.

RIGHT: A *devata* door guardian, at the eastern entrance to the main sanctuary at the third level.
BELOW: The many faces on the sanctuary towers of the second and third levels of the temple.
OPPOSITE PAGE: A general view of the Bayon, which is the only temple in Angkor with a round central tower.

Bayon - Bas-reliefs

Most of the bas-reliefs dealing with episodes from the history of Cambodia during Jayavarman VII's reign on the Bayon's outer gallery wall consist of processions and battles. However, the lower sections of these reliefs show scenes in a forest setting and, less frequently, in villages or towns: in palaces, at a market or on the banks of a watercourse. These reliefs are of great interest for the information they provide on the everyday life of the Khmers, but their anecdotal character tells us little about the significance of the scenes they portray.

LEFT, TOP TO BOTTOM: Reliefs on the southern outer gallery: a pig fight; a cockfight; market scenes.

ABOVE, TOP: A temple ceremony on the eastern outer gallery.

ABOVE: The southern interior gallery. An important dignitary prostrates himself before a statue of Vishnu. The bas-reliefs with mythological subjects on the interior gallery wall deal with many Vaishnavite themes, notably scenes from the life of Krishna on the southern side of the temple, and naval combats on the western side.

OPPOSITE PAGE, TOP: Scenes from naval battles between Khmers and Chams, the latter wearing helmets that cover their necks, are found on the southern external gallery.

OPPOSITE PAGE, BELOW: A military parade on the eastern external gallery.

Daily life of the Khmers during the reign of Jayavarman VII

As with the Baphuon and Angkor Wat, the Bayon has a notable set of narrative bas-reliefs. These frequently unfinished compositions are located on the two concentric enclosures of the temple, on the first and second levels of the pyramid. The external enclosure gallery—the first a visitor penetrates in visiting the temple—presents a series of scenes relating to the history of Cambodia following Jayavarman VII's reconquest of the country and the defeat of the Chams. The bas-reliefs on the interior gallery walls are devoted to scenes relating explicitly to Hinduism. In this Buddhist temple, they could reflect a form of syncretism of the kind often found in Khmer monuments, notably at the time of Jayavarman VII, but they could equally represent a decoration of the temple carried out by one or other of his immediate successors. The somewhat simplified style of some of the panels would seem to bear out this hypothesis. Generally, the composition and execution of the Bayon's bas-reliefs are less sophisticated than those found at Angkor Wat. Here the scenes are easier to understand and doubtless more attractive, mainly because of their often anecdotal character.

Elephant Terrace, Phimeanakas, Royal Palace

The arrangement of the Royal Square

The vast site of the Royal Palace, immediately to the north of the Baphuon, was surrounded by a five-metre-high laterite wall from the end of the 10th century. Accessed through five *gopura* of modest size, the palace compound, whose wooden buildings have disappeared, was screened by a wall and was the location for the small Phimeanakas temple, thought to be a kind of royal chapel. According to the Chinese traveller Zhou Daguan, who spent several months at Angkor at the end of the 13th century, this was where the ruler went each evening to couple with a serpent spirit in the form of a woman, so magically assuring the prosperity and peace of the kingdom. From the Elephant Terrace, constructed in front of the palace by Jayavarman VII and subsequently modified several times, the ruler and his court, once again according to Zhou Daguan, reviewed the processions and magnificent festivals that took place in front of the palace.

PREVIOUS PAGES: The Elephant Terrace occupies more than 300 metres on the western side of the Royal Square.
RIGHT: The Phimeanakas temple-mountain cannot easily be linked to a particular reign. Nevertheless, it is possible to attribute the vaulted gallery in sandstone, the first of its kind at Angkor, to the reign of Suryavarman I.
BELOW: The eastern *gopura* of the Royal Palace. Here, in 1011, Suryavarman I inscribed the oath sworn by his officials when he ascended the throne.

Terrace of the Leper King

A site for royal cremations?

As was the case with the Elephant Terrace, the Terrace of the Leper King, located beyond it, was constructed by Jayavarman VII and later modified. This terrace owes its name to a statue of unknown date of the god Yama which previously sat on top of the terrace. It is now in the National Museum in Phnom Penh. As the statue was covered with lichen, local inhabitants thought it represented a king who had contracted leprosy after having been splashed by the blood of one of his counsellors whom he had just killed. In his haste to be cured, the ruler ordered the death of the young ascetic who had come to heal him and went to his grave afflicted by the disease which had become incurable. The legend aside, this terrace is considered as a possible site for royal cremations in terms of its iconography and its location to the north of the palace. A similar location north of the modern palace in Phnom Penh is used for funeral rites accorded kings or prominent members of the royal family.

RIGHT: The statue of the 'Leper King' which gave the terrace its name is now in the National Museum in Phnom Penh.
BELOW: The Terrace of the Leper King seen from the northern stairway of the Elephant Terrace. Seven levels of mythical beings and minor divinities with fierce appearances provide the decoration for this unusual construction.

Preah Palilay, Preah Pithu,
North and South Khleang, Prasat Suor Prat

RIGHT: The Preah Palilay temple (13th–14th centuries) is one of the few temples at Angkor where the iconography is strictly related to Lesser Vehicle Buddhism.

TOP, RIGHT: With a rectangular form, the South Khleang is more simple and smaller than the North Khleang and seems to date from a slightly later period. The oath sworn by the officials when Suryavarman I mounted the throne was engraved here, as it also was in the eastern *gopura* of the Royal Palace.

BOTTOM, LEFT: Temple U of the Preah Pithu group. The five monuments making up this group are part of the small number of foundations at Angkor constructed after the reign of Jayavarman VII.

BOTTOM, RIGHT: In the foreground are two of the strange Prasat Suor Prat monuments constructed in laterite and topped by corbel vaults. In the background, the North Khleang has been altered at a later date by the construction of a superstructure of false storeys covering its central section. As with the South Khleang, the roofing was originally in wood covered with tiles.

A range of temples around the Royal Square

Situated northwest of the royal terraces, Preah Palilay is one of the few temples at Angkor linked to Theravada Buddhism. The sanctuary, constructed on top of a high base with several levels, is in a ruinous state but its eastern *gopura* has very interesting pediments showing various scenes from the life of the Buddha. The eastern region of the Royal Square is occupied by a group of monuments of varied styles. The religious affiliation of most of these monuments remains uncertain. The 12 Prasat Suor Prat—built in laterite and known as the 'Towers of the Cord Dancers'—sheltered a series of images of the god Vishnu. The North and South Khleang, which are very poorly named since the word means 'store-house', are atypical examples of Khmer religious architecture and cannot be identified precisely. The five temples of the Preah Pitu group are interesting for having been built at a late date—after Jayavarman VII's reign—and for re-using parts of older temples, or of copying decorative styles from earlier periods, although sometimes not very faithfully.

So one can see some poorly proportioned *devata* in the Banteay Srei and Bayon styles at temple U; some *devata* in the Angkor Wat style, enriched by ornamentation in the Bayon style, at temple T; and some late images (16th century?) of Buddha and his monks at temple X.

▲ Baphuon

The most audacious temple-mountain at Angkor

By virtue of its height, this temple-mountain, situated immediately to the north of the Bayon, between that temple and the Royal Palace, is one of the most impressive monuments at Angkor. This five-tiered pyramid, crowned by a unique Shaivite sanctuary, was founded by King Udayadityavarman II in the third quarter of the 11th century. The sides are steep, a significant issue in carrying out conservation of the monument. For the first time at Angkor several vaulted enclosure galleries, built in sandstone, were constructed on the pyramid itself—on the first, third and fifth levels. It appears that the giant reclining Buddha on the western façade was built in the 16th century. This is evidence of the importance of construction carried out at Angkor after the Angkorian period and, as with Angkor Wat and Phnom Bakheng, the transformation of these Hindu temples into Buddhist sanctuaries.

One of the special characteristics of the Baphuon is the small bas-relief narrative panels, mostly found on the walls of the *gopura* of the second enclosure gallery on the pyramid's third level. Previewing the masterly compositions found at Angkor Wat and the Bayon, these simple and lively scenes present themes drawn from Indian epics (*Mahabharata* and *Ramayana*) or from the life of Krishna, as well as splendid depictions of animals.

OPPOSITE PAGE
TOP, RIGHT: Viewed from the eastern *gopura* of the fourth enclosure, the Baphuon pyramid is seen here being restored.
LEFT: Details of the bas-reliefs from *gopura* II, southeast corner.
BOTTOM, RIGHT: Rama killing the demon Marica, in a scene from the *Ramayana*; *gopura* II west, eastern face.
THIS PAGE
TOP, LEFT: Two wild boars face each other.
CENTRE, LEFT: *Gopura* III east, northern side. In a scene from the *Mahabharata*, Duhshasana humiliates Draupadi.
TOP, RIGHT: *Gopura* II east, southeastern corner. Various scenes from the epics. The series of panels on the right (shown in detail on the opposite page) describes very precisely a tale from the *Mahabharata*: the confrontation in the mountains between Arjuna and Shiva, disguised as a hunter (*kirata*).
BOTTOM: *Gopura* II west, eastern face. Scenes from the *Ramayana*, showing the Battle of Lanka between Rama's monkey allies and the *rakshasa*. On the left of the middle level the *rakshasa* are trying to awaken one of their number, the terrible and powerful Kumbhakarna.

From its foundation under Yashovarman I at the end of the 9th century, until the reign of Jayavarman VII at the end of the 12th century, the Khmer capital was progressively endowed with a great many monuments. Apart from its framework of religious architecture, and its infrastructure linked to the economic life of the city—the various *baray*, a network of canals for irrigation and, in some cases, transport—we scarcely have any idea of what the rest of the city looked like. Was settlement grouped in a very localised fashion or, to the contrary, dispersed and extensive? What was the

AROUND ANGKOR THOM
The area around Angkor Thom is rich in monuments from all periods

size of the forest cover and of cultivated areas? Excavations undertaken recently should provide important information on Angkor Thom itself, but it will be necessary to wait before the area around it is more precisely understood. If we presume that the temple-mountains were the central points about which the city was organised, the city's centre, after it was first established around Phnom Bakheng at the end of the 9th century, relocated around the Pre Rup temple, founded by King Rajendravarman in 961, around the middle of the 10th century. The eastern region of the Angkor complex, in addition to Rajendravarman's temples such as the Eastern Mebon and Pre Rup, is the location of a range of monuments from the same period. These include the temple of Bat Chum, a Buddhist foundation established by the important dignitary Kavindrarimathana, and an earlier foundation on the site of the temple of Banteay Kdei that could date back to the 9th century, but which was modified by the creation of Srah Srang. In a less clear fashion, the Ta Keo temple (last quarter of the 10th century) could also have been the centre of the city, but only for a very short time, since, following the accession to power of Suryavarman I in 1010, the centre once again seems to have been located in the region covered

by the first Angkorian city. Neither archeology nor epigraphy has so far provided convincing proof of any further change to the city's location and the construction of the stone walls of Angkor Thom firmly linked the capital to all or part the city founded by Yashovarman I. With our present knowledge—and not knowing the overall structure of the Angkor complex, but assuming an extensive urban network that was certainly very dense and full of activity—we have to consider the major foundations of the 12th and 13th centuries as temples that were established wherever land was available in a region already extensively occupied. In an area where land represented the main source of wealth, as is still the case today, the construction of temples would certainly have had to take account of the requirements of the economic system. If the eastern region of Angkor had been the favoured area for the construction of religious foundations during the second half of the 10th century, donors showed a preference for the northern region during Jayavarman VII's time. There are many temples in the Bayon style in this area, including those linked to Jayavarman VII himself, built after he had used up available areas in the previously inhabited parts of the capital: Ta Prohm, founded in 1186; Banteay Kdei, which he expanded; and Srah Srang which he refurbished. He also founded the majestic Preah Khan temple in 1191, on the site of his victory over the Chams at the time of the reconquest of Angkor, and built the Northern Baray—the Jayatataka—with the Neak Pean temple at its centre.

Among the monuments along what used to be called the 'grand circuit' particular attention should be paid to several temples whose styles are similar to Angkor Wat and which, as a result, are dated to the first half of the 12th century. These are Thommanon and Chau Say Tevoda which are close to each other and to the road leading to the Royal Palace. After the construction of the wall around Angkor Thom, this road passed under the Gate of Victory. Attention should also be given to the temple of Banteay Samre, a little apart from the main complex to the east.

Ta Keo, Chau Say Tevoda, Thommanon

The temples immediately to the east of Angkor Thom

We do not know the exact date of the Ta Keo temple. Work on its construction must have begun in Jayavarman V's reign and finished, without being fully completed, under his immediate successors. It appears that work on it was interrupted when lightning struck the building during its construction. Was it then thought no longer fit for the function that it had been going to fulfil? Whatever the reasons for its not being completed, Ta Keo is, of all the Khmer temples, the least finished and so provides a precise idea of the construction methods used, which involved the carefully dressed stones being assembled in a neatly jointed fashion. Thommanon and Chau Say Tevoda, two temples in the Angkor Wat style, are decorated in an iconographically rich manner, notably the pediments, lintels and the bases of pilasters.

BELOW: The eastern side of Ta Keo. The second of the five tiers of the temple has the earliest known example of a continuous gallery.

OPPOSITE PAGE

TOP, LEFT: Attributed to the first half of the 12th century, the temple of Chau Say Tevoda, seen here before its recent restoration, appears to date a little later than Thommanon. The sanctuary tower and the rectangular hall in front of it are decorated with beautiful *devata*.

TOP, RIGHT: Thommanon temple, built in the first half of the 12th century, consists of a sanctuary tower with an outer hall and porch in front of it; a rectangular building of the kind called a 'library', whose real function is unknown; and two *gopura*, one in the east, the other in the west, set in the outer wall which is now almost totally destroyed.

BOTTOM, RIGHT: In contrast to Chau Say Tevoda, Thommanon only has *devata* at the level of its sanctuary tower. Perfectly preserved on the southern side of the temple, they have the same outstanding beauty as those found at Angkor Wat.

Ta Prohm

A temple in its 'natural state'

With the construction of Ta Prohm, Jayavarman VII began a series of religious foundations whose size resembled that of an actual town. Consecrated in 1186, an image of the Buddhist goddess Prajnaparamita was worshipped in this temple 'for the spiritual well-being of the mother of the king'. Like most other foundations from Jayavarman VII's reign, important additions were made to the temple shortly after the original building was completed, which has resulted in a particularly dense and complex layout. In the central sanctuary, which may not have been completed, there is a series of holes in the sandstone blocks which would have been used, as at Preah Khan, to fix decorative plaques, probably in gilded bronze. The stele marking the temple's foundation states that Ta Prohm was the administrative centre for 102 hospitals, either founded or restored by the king.

OPPOSITE PAGE

TOP: A standing *devata* in the Bayon style.

BOTTOM: The northeast corner of the first enclosure gallery. On the right is the north porch of the central sanctuary's forecourt whose building blocks are only roughly finished. The large trees that the restorers have left in this monument allow a visitor to gain an idea of what the Western discoverers saw in the 19th century.

THIS PAGE

ABOVE: The many galleries and passages in Jayavarman VII's monuments were necessary to shelter the large number of images. Today, the pedestals that once supported these images are scattered throughout the temple.

RIGHT, TOP: The most famous and dramatic tree roots at Ta Prohm are found at the northwest corner of the eastern *gopura* of the fourth enclosure.

RIGHT, CENTRE: The decorative style of the 'Halls of Dancers' in Jayavarman VII's temples suggests they were added a little after the monuments' original construction. The peripheral walls of the dancers' hall at Ta Prohm are still standing, while the inside is blocked with stone fallen from the collapsed roofs.

RIGHT, BOTTOM: In the almost inextricable chaos of sandstone building blocks inside Ta Prohm, the roof of this gallery has been replaced by a huge tree root.

Banteay Kdei, Srah Srang

An ancient site renovated by Jayavarman VII

The temple of Banteay Kdei is built on the site of an older monument and remained occupied by Buddhist monks long after the reign of Jayavarman VII. More open than the other monuments of the same period, Banteay Kdei is also better preserved. In front of the temple, to the east, is the Srah Srang, which along with the Western Baray is the only important artificial Angkorian reservoir still holding water. Jayavarman VII endowed it with a magnificent landing place decorated with lions and balustrades in the form of *naga*.

PREVIOUS PAGES: The Srah Srang in the early morning. BELOW: The manner in which the eastern *gopura* of the third enclosure of Banteay Kdei is constructed recalls, in a more modest fashion, the arrangement of the *gopura* giving access to the central sections of Ta Prohm and Preah Khan.

OPPOSITE PAGE
TOP, LEFT: The central sanctuary tower of Prasat Kravan contains three monumental bas-reliefs showing the god Vishnu in his various manifestations.
TOP, RIGHT: Above the image of the eight-armed Vishnu, the crocodile represents the 'Great Bear' constellation.
CENTRE: Lakshmi on the west

wall of the north sanctuary.
CENTRE, RIGHT: Durga on the south wall of the north sanctuary.
BOTTOM, LEFT: Vishnu Trivikrama and Vishnu in cosmic form with eight arms, on the south and west walls of the central sanctuary.
BOTTOM, RIGHT: Vishnu riding his mount, Garuda, on the north wall of the central sanctuary.

Internal bas-reliefs

The Vaishnavite temple of Prasat Kravan shelters a magnificent series of internal bas-reliefs in the central and extreme northern sanctuary towers which are part of an ensemble of five *prasat* constructed on a single terrace. Founded by a family of high officials, this brick temple was consecrated in 921.

Pre Rup, Eastern Mebon

Two elegant temples from the middle of the 10th century

Founded in 953 and 961 by Rajendravarman, the Eastern Mebon, at the centre of the Eastern Baray, and Pre Rup, a little to the south, differ from each other by the fact that the first is not really in the form of a stepped pyramid. Their decoration—lintels and columns in sandstone—are very finely executed. In each, the five main sanctuaries and the auxiliary buildings in brick—little temples, libraries, *gopura*—were covered with a coating of stucco, with some traces still existing at Pre Rup.

PREVIOUS PAGES: The temple of Pre Rup shows its majestic silhouette surrounded by rice fields.

RIGHT: At the corners of the two terraces making up the base of the Eastern Mebon, elephants—symbolising the earth and the underworld—guarantee the stability of the monument.

BELOW: At the Eastern Mebon, as with Pre Rup, the five main sanctuaries are arranged on a terrace in a quincuncial form.

Banteay Samre

A Buddhist foundation from the Angkor Wat period

Despite a largely Hindu iconography, with many scenes drawn from the epics on the pediments, lintels or the bases of pilasters, Banteay Samre is a Buddhist monument comparable to the famous temple of Phimai (late 11th–early 12th century) in modern Thailand. The decoration of this temple is ravishing, particularly on the multi-curved pediments of the *gopura* of both the outer and inner enclosures. Shortly after the temple was constructed important modifications were made to the level of the eastern entrance and to the interior enclosure. The latter's transformation into a gallery somewhat cramps the buildings located inside it: a sanctuary tower with rectangular antechamber and two libraries.

BELOW, LEFT: The southeastern corner of the inner gallery enclosure. In the centre the upper section of the sanctuary, with its arch-like appearance, is very characteristic of the Angkor Wat architectural style.
BELOW, RIGHT: The outer gallery enclosure consists of carefully worked laterite walls with sandstone pillars running along its inner side.
BOTTOM, LEFT: *Gopura* I, south. As with all other buildings at Banteay Samre, this *gopura* shows the distinctive decorative form of a multi-curved pediment. First appearing at Banteay Srei, this then became a characteristic of Khmer monuments. The narrative scenes sculpted in high relief are of an equivalent quality to the pediments at Angkor Wat. They are more obvious here because of the modest proportions of the temple.
BOTTOM, RIGHT: An aerial view of the temple from the southwest.

Preah Khan

The city of 'The Victorious Royal Emblem'

Preah Khan was founded in 1191 by Jayavarman VII on the spot where he gained a decisive victory over the Chams, and has the dimensions of a town. The modern-day name for this great temple corresponds to the ancient name of the monument incised on its foundation stele: Preah Khan, 'Sacred Sword' also known as Jayashri, 'The Victorious Royal Emblem'. This similarity of name is unusual as, in general, there is no connection between the names by which temples are known today and the names given them at the time they were built. In this temple the king consecrated, in addition to 515 other statues, an image of the *bodhisattva* Lokeshvara (one of the most important divinities of Mahayana Buddhism) to the spiritual well-being of his father in the afterworld, just as he had done with an image of Prajnaparamita for his mother five years earlier at Ta Prohm. While Preah Khan does not have towers bearing faces, as is the case with most of the other important foundations at the end of the 12th century, it shares with Angkor Thom and the great provincial temple of Banteay Chmar spectacular parapets formed by giants supporting the body of a *naga* across the moats which surround it.

RIGHT, TOP: *Gopura* III west, seen from outside the third enclosure.
RIGHT, BOTTOM: The upper section of the 'Hall of Dancers', in the eastern part of the third enclosure, has an outstanding frieze of dancing female divinities beneath a series of niches that previously held images of the Buddha.

OPPOSITE PAGE

TOP, LEFT: One of the many *garuda*, a mythical animal that is half man and half bird of prey, overpowering two *naga*, set in the wall of the fourth enclosure. These sculptures refer to the *garuda* who came to the aid of the *deva* (gods) and frightened away the *asura* (demons) when they attempted to assault and seize Mount Meru. There is an allusion, here, to the battles waged by the Khmers (represented by the *deva*) against the Chams (the *asura*), on the spot where Preah Khan now stands.

TOP, RIGHT: Within the third enclosure, to the north of the 'Hall of Dancers'; the purpose of this hall, with its rounded columns, remains uncertain. A similar building, but with square columns, exists in the same relative position at Banteay Kdei and Ta Prohm.

BOTTOM: *Gopura* I south, southern side. In the background it is possible to see the *stupa* which today occupies the inner sanctum of the sanctuary tower.

Banteay Prei, Prasat Prei, Ta Som, Krol Ko

Minor temples from the time of Jayavarman VII

Various temples from the reign of Jayavarman VII are scattered around the north of the Angkor complex. Lacking any distinctive individuality, these monuments from Jayavarman's time are characteristically decorated without much attention to detail. Here, as is also the case with the major temples, one encounters an amazing effort to simplify the work of the sculptors. So, there are curious false windows with balusters on a curtain-wall background, eliminating the need to sculpt the balusters in the round and also for their entire height, since only a third of each one is visible. To the east of the Jayatataka—the Northern Baray—the small temple of Ta Som is notable for the quality of its sculptures and the fine faces on its outer *gopura*.

RIGHT, TOP: Ta Som, eastern side of the first enclosure.
RIGHT, CENTRE: The sanctuary of Prasat Krol Ko, viewed from the southeast.
RIGHT, BOTTOM: Prasat Prei, a general view from the southeast.
BELOW: Banteay Prei, eastern side of the first enclosure.

A representation of the mythical Lake Anavatapta in the Himalayas

Inspired by descriptions in the sacred texts, Khmer architecture very often produced images of mythical locations, such as Mount Meru, Mount Kailasa, and so on. Neak Pean, built on an artificial island in the centre of the Northern Baray, the Jayatataka, is a very faithful representation of Lake Anavatapta, whose waters, which are the last to dry up at the end of a cosmic era, are believed to possess curative qualities. According to Buddhist cosmology, the four great rivers watering the world have their source in the lake, and flow from four gargoyles in the form of animal heads. The single sanctuary at Neak Pean is built at the centre of a complex system of interconnecting pools.

ABOVE, LEFT: The horse, Balaha, an incarnation of the *bodhisattva* Lokeshvara, rescuing shipwrecked sailors (the souls of believers seeking salvation).
ABOVE, RIGHT: One of the four gargoyles allowing water to flow from the central pool at Neak Pean into the surrounding pools. This human head in the monument's eastern section replaces the bull's head described in the Buddhist texts. The three other gargoyles are a lion's head, to the south; a horse's head to the west; and an elephant's head to the north.
LEFT: The circular base of the sanctuary is ringed by two *naga*—symbols of water—whose tails are intertwined. Neak Pean means 'Entwined Serpents'.

Several major sites are located within a radius of 15 to 40 kilometres around Siem Reap, the little town from which one visits the monuments and whose development and prosperity today depend on tourism. In Angkorian times these satellite sites were the temples of towns that were probably modest in size, such as Ishvarapura with its magnificent temple of Banteay Srei, or sanctuaries and holy places which were somewhat isolated geographically but were, nevertheless, an integral part of the ancient Angkorian network. In this latter category were the

AWAY FROM ANGKOR
Important sites around Angkor and in the provinces

temples of Phnom Kulen, the river of a thousand *linga*, as well as the monuments at Phnom Bok and Phnom Krom. The marvellous buildings (Preah Ko, Bakong and others) of Hariharalaya/Roluos, the capital which preceded Angkor as the leading city in the kingdom, foreshadowed in many ways the great temples of Yashodharapura.

If the Angkor region is exceptionally rich architecturally, Cambodia's historic provinces should not be disregarded. Throughout the country—but also in Laos and Thailand, for ancient Cambodia occupied a much larger area than the present-day country—there are monuments of greater or lesser importance dating from all periods.

Starting with the pre-Angkorian period, a time when several independent kingdoms existed side by side, various groups of monuments were constructed. With the passage of centuries, these sites were maintained and sometimes altered in accordance with religious changes in the country: at Angkor Borei and Phnom Da, in the modern southern province of Takeo, where the oldest Cambodian royal cities have been found; Wat Phu in Laos, a very important Shaivite holy place since at least the 5th century; Sambor Prei Kuk,

in Kompong Thom province, the capital of Ishanavarman I at the beginning of the 7th century; Han Chei, a little-known site in Kompong Cham province which was certainly of great importance in the 7th century; not to mention the very many small isolated temples such as Prasat Andet (late 7th century), Prasat Phum Prasat (806), and Prasat Kompong Preah (8th century). Temples from the pre-Angkorian period are generally built in brick, with sandstone reserved for decorative elements such as door frames. The thickness of the masonry— but also the fact that many of these monuments were re-dedicated to the Buddhist faith around the 14th century and then continuously maintained— explains why a fairly large number of these ancient buildings has survived until now.

From the beginning of the Angkorian period an even larger number of religious foundations were built throughout the Cambodian empire. Some of these were important cities. Such was the case with Koh Ker, located 100 kilometres to the northeast of Angkor and the capital in the second quarter of the 10th century under Jayavarman IV and his successor. Among the multitude of monuments from this period it is worth mentioning Suryavarman I's important foundations at Phnom Chisor, south of Phnom Penh; at Preah Vihear, located on the Dangrek mountain chain on the frontier between Cambodia and Thailand; and Wat Ek Phnom and Wat Baset in the Battambang region. Among the temples built by Suryavarman II, or by some of his great officials, were those at Wat Phu and Beng Mealea, while Jayavarman VII founded or completed a range of striking and very large sanctuaries, veritable cities in some cases, such as the temples of Preah Khan of Kompong Svay, Ta Prohm of Bati, and Banteay Chmar. This last great complex, with its towers decorated with faces, causeways lined by giants and narrative bas-reliefs, reminds us of Angkor Thom and allows us to realise how very rich and important is the range of Cambodia's historic monuments and how deserving they are of the greatest interest.

The Roluos Group

Bakong, Preah Ko, Lolei, a first accomplishment

Some 15 kilometres to the east of Siem Reap is an important group of monuments which are among the earliest in the Angkor region. While the principal temples, known as the Roluos group from the name of a small present-day village around which they spread, can be dated to the last quarter of the 9th century (the reign of Indravarman, 877 to at least 886), some buildings are from an earlier period. These include Prasat Prei Monti and Prasat Trapeang Phong, among others.

The Roluos group, the ancient city of Hariharalaya and one of the last residences of Jayavarman II, provides an opportunity to study the typology of the great Khmer royal foundations, as they would later develop at Angkor itself. There is a *baray,* the Indratataka or the pool of Indra (varman), which is now dry; an ancestor temple, Preah Ko; and a state temple, Bakong.

Lolei, the temple to the ancestors, built by Yashovarman in 893, was the last important foundation built before the capital moved to be centred around Phnom Bakheng.

ABOVE: Southern door jamb of the southwestern sanctuary tower of the Lolei temple. Inscriptions dealing with the consecration of the divinities found within the sanctuary towers are often located on their door frames. These inscriptions also deal with practical matters for the foundation, such as provision of subsistence, lists of servants, and so on. These inscriptions in Sanskrit or Old Khmer display calligraphy of a fine standard, which evolves over time.

LEFT: The six brick sanctuary towers of Preah Ko (879), which are arranged in two rows, have preserved some important traces of marvellous stucco decoration. A recent restoration, necessitated by the building's fragile state, has resulted in some disfigurement of the monument.

RIGHT: Bakong, a pyramid of five levels, seen from the east. The consecration stele for the images set up by Indravarman at the Bakong temple bears the date 881, but the decoration on some of the structures of this building appears older. As for the sanctuary tower, it is a reconstruction from the late 11th century or very early 12th century.

▲ Banteay Srei

A magnificent home for the god Shiva

Some 30 kilometres northeast of Siem Reap, the sanctuaries of the temple of Ishvarapura are found in the forest at the heart of a complex made up of three concentric enclosures, the third containing a moat, and approached from the east by a long causeway after passing through a cruciform *gopura*.

Consecrated in 967, the principal images are in the three *prasat* of the first enclosure, which also is the location for two libraries with wonderful multi-curved pediments covered with rich narrative decoration. The temple is notable for its pink sandstone, but above all for the exceptional virtuosity of its decoration: every leaf and petal has been incised with a jeweller's skill. The delicacy of this work is matched by the highest degree of invention, in terms of iconography, whether in the sections that deal with the narratives themselves, or in the elements of the decoration that surround them. The suppleness in the modelling of the male and female guardians of the doors of the sanctuary towers is unique in Khmer art, as is the case with their smiling, youthful faces. The central sanctuary tower and the southern tower are dedicated to Shiva. Vishnu was worshipped in the northern tower.

The very much reduced scale of the temple gives Banteay Srei the character of a 'miniature'. It is possible to observe here a progressive reduction in the size of the buildings, according to a striking logic, from the exterior of the complex to its interior.

RIGHT, TOP: The most celebrated work of art from Banteay Srei is a representation of Umamaheshvara—Shiva and his consort Parvati—which is conserved in Phnom Penh's National Museum. It was originally housed in the small western *gopura*, constructed in brick, within the temple's first enclosure.

RIGHT, BOTTOM: The temple's first two enclosures, as seen across the moat.

OPPOSITE PAGE

TOP, LEFT: The decorative friezes of leaves and flowers sit below the cornices of the various buildings.

TOP, RIGHT: The multi-curved pediments represent one of the many architectural innovations at Banteay Srei. The eastern pediment of the northern library shows the burning of the forest of Khandava, an episode from the *Mahabharata*.

BOTTOM: The central sanctuaries.

Phnom Bok, Phnom Krom

Two temples dedicated to the Hindu triad

Almost 'twins', the two monuments of Phnom Bok and Phnom Krom are located, respectively, northeast and southwest of Angkor. They were built either at the very end of the 9th, or the very beginning of the 10th, century. Each situated on one of the rare hills of the region, these temples are dedicated to the *trimurti*, the three great Hindu gods: Shiva, Vishnu and Brahma. Both monuments each consist of three sanctuary towers on a single terrace, and have four libraries facing the central towers. Although lacking inscriptions, it is quite clear that, in one manner or another, they form part of the ambitious architectural program of Yashovarman's reign.

TOP: Wind erosion has removed almost all of the decoration from the three sandstone sanctuaries of Phnom Krom.

CENTRE: The three *prasat* of Phnom Bok, seen from the southeast. Despite the collapse of the upper sections of the temple, this monument provides some of the finest and best preserved examples of ornamental sculpture in the Bakheng style (late 9th to early 10th centuries).

BOTTOM, LEFT: Detail of a pedestal for the statue of Vishnu in the northern sanctuary tower of Phnom Krom. The images of Garuda, the god's mount, are sculpted in dynamic poses on the bas-relief of one of the upper mouldings.

BOTTOM, RIGHT: A pedestal in circular form for the statue of Brahma in the southern sanctuary tower of Phnom Krom. The decorative section around its middle is ornamented with geese, the god's mount, depicted side on and with their wings spread.

Kbal Spean, Phnom Kulen

Sacred mountains and rivers

The large number and varied character of remains scattered over an area of about 30 square kilometres northeast of Angkor make Phnom Kulen—a sandstone plateau of medium height reaching some 500 metres at its highest point—one of the most important archeological sites in the Angkor region. Historically, it was here that Jayavarman II was anointed as a *cakravartin*, 'The turner of the wheel', the king of kings.

The region was important both historically and economically. The sites of several kilns bear witness to the presence of an important ceramics industry, while the substantial forest cover on the plateau and its productive quarries furnished large quantities of material for the builders of Angkor.

The watercourses that flow down from the plateau played an important role in filling the *baray* and also took on a sacred character. The beds of some of the rivers were the location for a mass of sculptures—*linga*, images of Vishnu reclining on the *naga* Ananta, representing eternity, and others—so that the water was in fact sanctified before flowing to fill the moats of the temples and irrigate the rice fields. The sites on Phnom Kulen correspond to almost the whole of the Angkorian period. Unfortunately many of them are today in a ruinous state, mostly because of theft.

RIGHT: Prasat Thma Dap, eastern side of the temple, first half of the 9th century.
BELOW, TOP LEFT: Southern lintel of Prasat Thma Dap. The head of the central monster (*kala*) is in the Kulen style from the early 9th century. This head was used often in the styles of later periods.
BELOW, BOTTOM LEFT: The river bed of Kbal Spean—literally 'bridgehead'—is sculpted with divine images: on the left, a *linga* in a sanctuary tower; and on the right, Vishnu reclining on the *naga* Ananta.
BOTTOM, RIGHT: Prasat O Paong, the eastern side of the temple, first half of the 9th century.

▲ Beng Mealea

A great Buddhist temple in the Angkor Wat style

The remains of Beng Mealea, which is still partly buried under vegetation, consist of an indescribable chaos of perfectly squared-off sandstone building blocks, with outstanding decoration dating from the first half of the 12th century.

Partially studied at various times, the monument, whose central section consists of three concentric enclosures, remains poorly known because of its ruined state.

Although the pediments of some buildings are sculpted with scenes from the *Ramayana*, and while Hindu iconographic themes are plentiful, Beng Mealea is quite clearly a Buddhist sanctuary, as is Banteay Samre, which is more or less contemporaneous. This is confirmed by the magnificent statue of the *bodhisattva* Lokeshvara (photographed right) found in the monument and today housed at the Angkor Conservancy.

RIGHT: Southeastern pavilion in the third enclosure.
BOTTOM: The northern library within the third enclosure.
OPPOSITE PAGE, TOP: The sanctuary tower of Prasat Preah Stung is the first-known example of a tower adorned with faces found in Cambodia.
OPPOSITE PAGE, BOTTOM: The central part of Preah Khan is an outstanding example of early 12th-century architecture.

Preah Khan of Kompong Svay

One of the largest provincial complexes at the height of the Angkorian period.

An inscription records the existence of a small religious foundation on the site of the vast temple of Preah Khan of Kompong Svay (modern province of Kompong Thom) dating from the first half of the 11th century.

The main section of this Buddhist complex, badly degraded by recent thefts, is in the Angkor Wat style. But other important buildings—Preah Damrei, Preah Thkol and Preah Stung—date from the reign of Jayavarman VII who, additionally, built a wall forming a square measuring five kilometres along each side with earth levees and moats. This wall was probably built after the construction of the *baray*, located beyond the main temple on the east.

Koh Ker

A transitory capital

For reasons that are still largely unknown, Jayavarman IV moved the court and the royal institutions to Koh Ker in 928. Until the return to Angkor following Rajendravarman's accession to the throne, Koh Ker was the capital of the kingdom. The site is made up of a *baray*—the Rahal—and a sizeable complex of striking monuments, some very large in size, such as Prasat Thom (The Great Prasat) dedicated to the god Shiva. This temple, built on an axial plan, has a majestic pyramid, the Prang, within an enclosure located at the rear of the main buildings. At its summit is a sanctuary that seems never to have been completed. The sculptures found at Koh Ker in the course of the first clearing operations are often colossal in size and sometimes depict figures in motion, something that has not been found in any other examples of Khmer sculpture. Many that were left on the site have sadly disappeared today.

RIGHT: The Prasat Kraham is the eastern *gopura* of the third enclosure of Prasat Thom. It houses various sculptures, notably an image of a dancing Shiva. The main fragments of this statue are today conserved in the National Museum in Phnom Penh.
BELOW: An aerial view of the Prang. On its summit was a *linga* on a monumental pedestal decorated with supporting lions.

A pre-Angkorian capital

The site of Sambor Prei Kuk, whose ancient name was Ishanapura, is the most important pre-Angkorian complex and the best-preserved in Cambodia. The three main groups (in the south, the oldest with inscriptions of Ishanavarman I, dating from the first quarter of the 7th century; in the centre, the most recent, probably dating from the 8th century; and in the north, contemporaneous with the southern group) are in the form of brick temples with various ground plans: square, rectangular and octagonal. The aesthetic quality and the iconographic richness of the decoration are remarkable. The remains of a *baray* have been found to the east of the site.

TOP: The two principal monuments of the southern group. On the right, tower S1 housed an image of Shiva in gold; on the left, tower S2 housed a sandstone dais on which was placed a silver statue of the bull, Nandi, the god's mount.
BOTTOM, LEFT: The octagonal temples at Sambor Prei Kuk are the only ones of their kind in Khmer architecture. As with the other monuments at the site, their walls are decorated with images showing the contemporary wooden architecture of the period.
BOTTOM, RIGHT: Temple N17 is the only monument in stone at Sambor Prei Kuk.

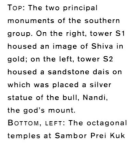

▲ Other temples

The rich heritage in the provinces

Emphasising the enduring fashion in which sacred sites
have been occupied since ancient times, it is not unusual
for Buddhist temples in modest villages to house old
Brahmanic monuments as is the case at Prasat Andet and
Prasat Phum Prasat. The large number of major provincial
foundations (Ta Prohm of Bati, south of Phnom Penh; or
Banteay Chmar, in the northwest of the country) and
various temples (such as Phimai in Thailand) testify to the
period when Cambodia's power extended over a large part
of mainland Southeast Asia. Some of these monuments
are built on exceptional sites. The main buildings of Wat
Phu in Laos are located on the slope of a mountain whose
summit is regarded as being the form of a *linga*.
Inscriptions, sculptures and monuments on the site date
from the 5th to the 13th centuries. This Shaivite temple,
later transformed into a Buddhist sanctuary, was an
important sacred site for ancient Cambodia. Preah Vihear,
built on a rocky promontory in the Dangrek Chain, has
structures dating back to the 11th century, as does the
temple built on the top of Phnom Chisor, south of Phnom
Penh. Finally, Prasat Phnom Da, located not far from
Angkor Borei in the south, is one of the few Cambodian
monuments constructed entirely in laterite. Magnificent
Vaishnavite statues from the pre-Angkorian period, and
now housed in the National Museum in Phnom Penh, were
found in this temple, which was built in the 12th century.

RIGHT, TOP: The central sanctuary at Phnom Chisor is reached
through a rectangular hallway with internal pillars characteristic of
the time of Suryavarman I (first half of the 11th century).
RIGHT, BOTTOM: Banteay Chmar, one of the most fascinating
temples in Cambodia, was built in the reign of Jayavarman VII at
the beginning of the 13th century. In addition to its towers
adorned with faces, it has a series of bas-reliefs very similar
to those at the Bayon.
OPPOSITE PAGE
TOP, LEFT: The Buddhist temple of Phimai in Thailand (late 11th
to early 12th centuries) is considered the oldest example of a
monument in the Angkor Wat style.
TOP, RIGHT: Preah Vihear, 11th century.
CENTRE, LEFT: The approach promenade, flanked by pools and
subsidiary buildings, leading to the main temple of Wat Phu in
Laos, seen from the sanctuary. Most of the structures visible today
date from the 11th and 12th centuries.
CENTRE, MIDDLE: Prasat Phum Prasat, beginning of the 8th century.
CENTRE, RIGHT: Prasat Andet, end of the 7th century.
BOTTOM, LEFT: Prasat Phnom Da, 12th century.
BOTTOM, RIGHT: A pediment showing the *bodhisattva* Lokeshvara at
Ta Prohm of Bati, late 12th to early 13th centuries.

Map of the Sites

1 Prasat Ak Yum

2 Western Mebon

3 Bayon

4 Phnom Bakheng

5 Angkor Wat

6 Ta Prohm

7 Banteay Kdei

8 Prasat Kravan

9 Srah Srang

10 Pre Rup

11 Eastern Mebon

12 Ta Som

13 Neak Pean

14 Krol Ko

15 Ta Keo

16 Prasat Prei

17 Chau Say Tevoda

18 Thommanon

19 Preah Khan

20 Banteay Prei

21 Kbal Spean

22 Banteay Srei

23 Phnom Kulen

24 Phnom Bok

25 Beng Mealea

26 Banteay Samre

27 Lolei

28 Bakong

29 Preah Ko

30 Prasat Prei Monti

31 Phnom Krom

32 Angkor Thom

Map not to scale

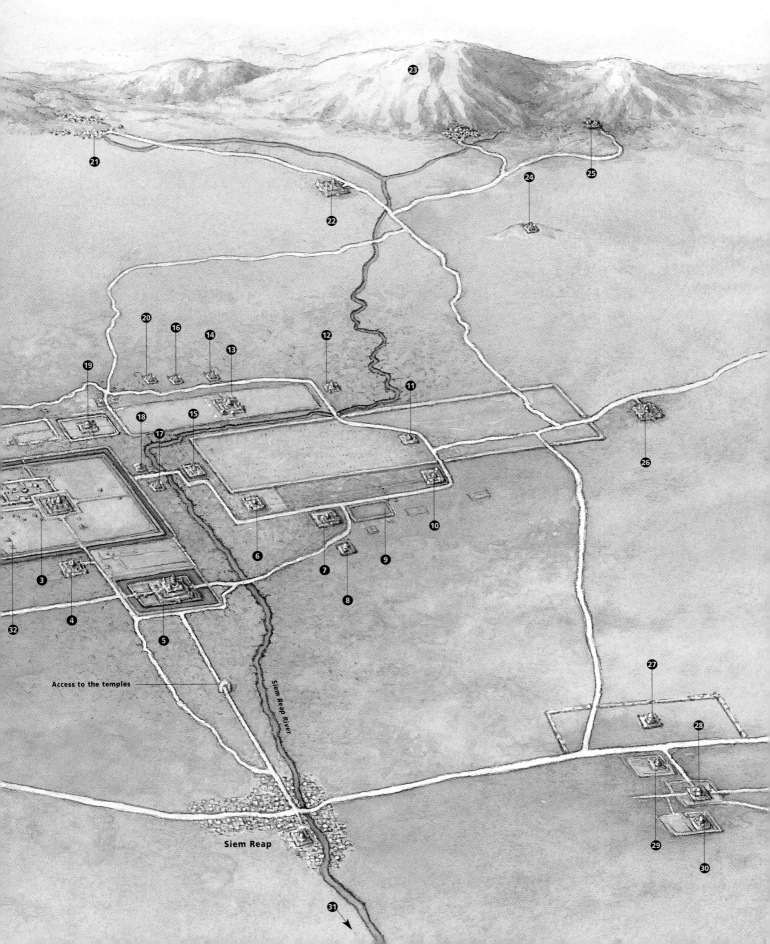

Access to the temples

Siem Reap River

Siem Reap

Map of Angkor Thom

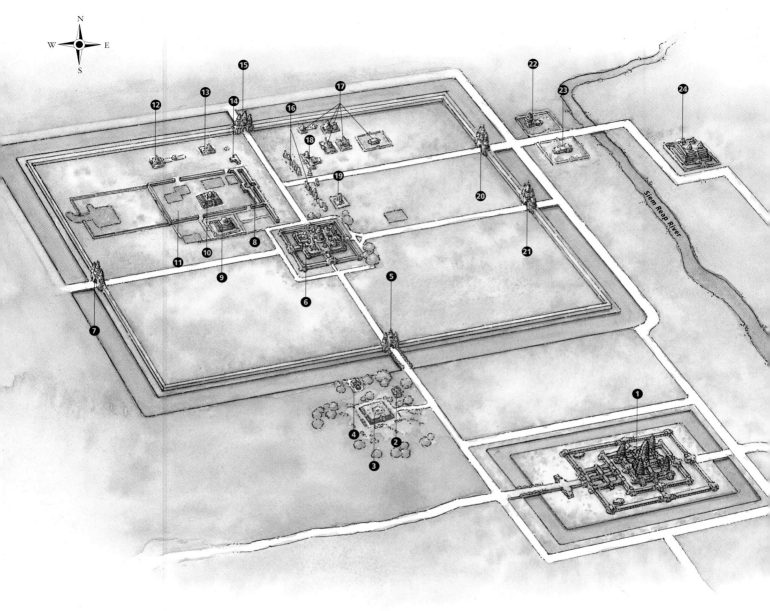

Map not to scale

1. Angkor Wat
2. Baksei Chamkrong
3. Phnom Bakheng
4. Prasat Bei
5. South Gate
6. Bayon
7. West Gate
8. Elephant Terrace
9. Baphuon
10. Phimeanakas
11. Royal Palace
12. Preah Palilay
13. Tep Pranam
14. Terrace of the Leper King
15. North Gate
16. Prasat Suor Prat
17. Preah Pithu
18. North Khleang
19. South Khleang
20. Gate of Victory
21. Gate of the Dead
22. Thommanon
23. Chau Say Tevoda
24. Ta Keo

RIGHT: Banteay Srei, c. 967, a detail on the eastern pediment of the eastern porch of the central sanctuary tower. Indra is seated on the three-headed elephant, Airavata.

apsara (Sanskrit): 'those who walk, or glide, on water', the term given to the celestial nymphs who appeared in the course of the churning the sea of milk. The name given to the minor feminine deities, whether dancing or not, sculpted on the walls of the monuments. (see *devata*)

baray (Khmer): a large reservoir of water surrounded by dykes and symbolically representing the cosmic ocean while providing irrigation for rice fields.

Brahmanism (or Hinduism): the Indian religion originating from the Vedic religion (Vedism) brought into the subcontinent by the Aryans towards the middle of the second millennium before the birth of Christ. In India, Vedism mingled with existing indigenous animist religions and cults linked to the underworld. In Brahmanism the supreme divine principle is linked to the particular attributes of individual gods: Shiva, Vishnu, and so on. The concept of time in India, and in 'Indianised' countries, is cyclical, with the soul of a believer progressing from existence to existence until it is finally united with the Universal Soul, the Creator, obtaining *moksha* (the liberation of the soul).

Buddhism: the religion founded in the 6th century BCE by Siddhartha Gautama, also known as Shakyamuni (the Sage of the Shakya) or more commonly the Buddha (the Enlightened One). As an alternative to the ritualised religious practices of Brahmanism (or Hinduism), Buddhism preaches a way of life in which the salvation of the soul—meaning an end to the cycle of reincarnation by entering *nirvana* (the state of not being born again)—can be achieved after many incarnations by means of meditation. Several forms of Buddhism developed from the original doctrine known as Theravada (the doctrine of the Elders) or Hinayana (Lesser Vehicle) which is practised in Cambodia today. From the beginning of our own era, Mahayana (Greater Vehicle) Buddhism introduced the idea of the *bodhisattva* (a being destined to become enlightened) coming to the aid of the faithful on their journey towards salvation. Beginning in the 7th and 8th centuries, Vajrayana (Diamond Vehicle) Buddhism, also known as Tantric Buddhism, offered deliverance from rebirth in a single existence through esoteric practices.

devata (Sanskrit): 'divinity', a term applied to the feminine deities of minor importance sculpted on the walls of the monuments (see *apsara*).

gopura (Sanskrit): 'city gate', refers to the access pavilions leading into the various enclosures of the monuments.

linga (Sanskrit): 'sign' or 'symbol', an abstract representation of the god Shiva in the form of a stylised phallus and incarnating the creative power of the god.

Mahabharata (Sanskrit): 'the Great Epic of the Bharata', the epic story which recounts the rivalry between the five Pandava brothers and their one hundred cousins, the Kauravas.

naga (Sanskrit): 'snake', a term used to describe all representations of the many-headed cobra.

prasat (Khmer): 'sanctuary tower'.

Ramayana (Sanskrit): 'the Epic of Rama', the epic story which recounts Rama's quest, undertaken with the aid of the monkey people, to recover his consort Sita, who had been kidnapped by the demon Ravana.

BIBLIOGRAPHY

This bibliography contains the titles of general works. In-depth articles may be found in the *Bulletin de l'Ecole française d'Extrême-Orient*, which has appeared regularly since 1901. More recent articles may be found in the journal *Udaya*, published by APSARA since 2000.

Bhattacharya, Kamaleswar, *Les religions brahmaniques dans l'ancien Cambodge d'après l'épigraphie et l'iconographie*, Publications de l'École française d'Extrême-Orient, vol. XLIX, Paris, 1961.

Boisselier, Jean, *Le Cambodge* (Manuel d'Archéologie d'Extrême-Orient. Première Partie, tome I), Picard, Paris, 1966.

Briggs, Laurence Palmer, *The Ancient Khmer Empire*, American Philosophical Society, Philadelphia, 1951.

Chou Ta-Kuan [Zhou Daguan], *Notes on the customs of Cambodia* (translated from Paul Pelliot's French edition by J. Gilman D'Arcy Paul), Social Science Association Press, Bangkok, 1967.

Clémentin-Ojha, Catherine and Manguin, Pierre-Yves, *Un siècle pour l'Asie – L'École française d'Extrême-Orient, 1898–2000*. Les Éditions du Pacifique et l'École française d'Extrême-Orient, Paris, 2001.

Coedès, George, *Inscriptions du Cambodge* (edited and translated into French), 8 vol., l'École française d'Extrême-Orient, collection de textes et documents sur l'Indochine, III, Hanoi-Paris, 1937–1966.

Coedès, George, *The Indianized States of Southeast Asia*, East–West Center Press, Honolulu, 1968.

Dagens, Bruno, *Angkor – Heart of an Asian Empire*, New Horizons, Thames and Hudson, London, 1995.

Dagens, Bruno, *Les Khmers*, Guides belles Lettres des Civilisations, Les Belles Lettres, Paris, 2003.

Dharma, Krishna, *Mahabharata: The Greatest Spiritual Epic of All Time*, Torchlight Publishing, 1999.

Dharma, Krishna, *Ramayana: India's Immortal Tale of Adventure, Love and Wisdom*, Torchlight Publishing, 2000.

Dumarçay, Jacques and Royère, Pascal, *Cambodian Architecture, Eighth to Thirteenth Centuries* (Handbook of Oriental Studies. Section Three. South-East Asia. Vol. XII), Brill, Leiden, 2001.

Glaize, Maurice, *Les monuments du groupe d'Angkor* (fourth edition with preface, notes and addenda by Jean Boisselier), Jean Maisonneuve, Paris, 1993.

Groslier, Bernard Philippe and Arthaud, Jacques, *Angkor, Art and Civilisation* (translated from the French by Eric Ernshaw Smith), Thames and Hudson, London, 1966.

Jacques, Claude and Freeman, Michael, *Angkor, Cities and Temples*, translated by Tom White, River Books, Bangkok, 2000.

Jessup, Helen Ibbitson and Zéphir, Thierry (eds) *Sculpture of Angkor and Ancient Cambodia – Millennium of Glory*, Thames and Hudson, London, 1997.

Le Bonheur, Albert, *Of Gods, Kings and Men*, Serinda, London, 1995.

Lunet de Lajonquière, Étienne, *Inventaire descriptif des monuments du Cambodge*, 3 volumes, Ernest Leroux, Paris, 1902–1911.

Mabbett, Ian and Chandler, David, *The Khmers*, Blackwell, Oxford, 1995.

Moore, Elisabeth and Siribhadra, Smitthi, *Palaces of the Gods: Khmer Art and Architecture in Thailand*, River Books, Bangkok, 1992.

Pou, Saveros, *Nouvelles inscriptions du Cambodge* (translated into French and edited), volumes I, II and III, l'École française d'Extrême-Orient, Paris, 1989 and 2001.

Roveda, Vittorio, *Sacred Angkor – The Carved Reliefs of Angkor Wat*, River Books, Bangkok, 2002.

Stern, Philippe, *Les monuments khmers du style du Bàyon et Jayavarman VII*, Publications du Musée Guimet, Recherches et documents d'art et d'archéologie, tome IX, Presses Universitaires de France, Paris, 1965.

Zéphir, Thierry, *Khmer – Lost Empire of Cambodia*, New Horizons, Thames and Hudson, London, 1998.